Hispanic Heritage

Hispanic Heritage

Title List

The Story of Latino Civil Rights

Fighting for Justice

by Miranda Hunter

Mason Crest Publishers

Philadelphia

Mason Crest Publishers Inc.

370 Reed Road

Broomall, Pennsylvania 19008

(866) MCP-BOOK (toll free)

First printing

1 2 3 4 5 6 7 8 9 10

Library of Congress Cataloging-in-Publication Data

Hunter, Miranda, 1977-

  The story of Latino civil rights : fighting for justice / by Miranda Hunter.

    p. cm. — (Hispanic heritage)

  Includes index.

  ISBN 1-59084-934-5 ISBN 1-59084-924-8 (series)

  1. Civil rights—United States—Juvenile literature. 2. Hispanic Americans—Juvenile literature. 3. Minorities—United States—Juvenile literature. I. Title. II. Hispanic heritage (Philadelphia, Pa.)

  JC599.U5H86 2005

  323.1168'073 —dc22

                                      2004020677

Produced by Harding House Publishing Service, Inc., Vestal, NY.

Interior design by Dianne Hodack.

Cover design by Dianne Hodack.

Printed and bound in the Hashemite Kingdom of Jordan.

4

Contents

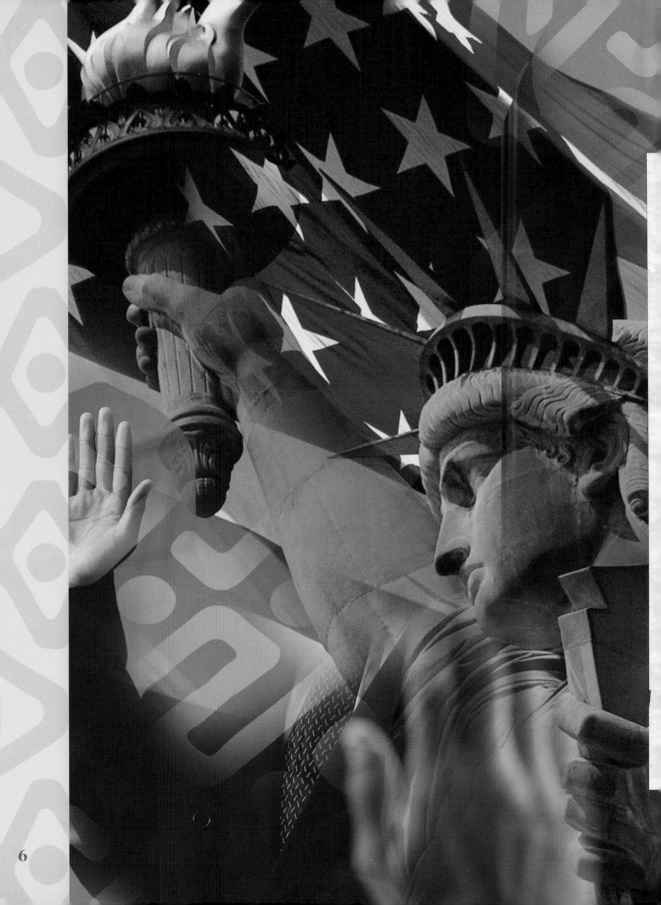

Introduction

by José E. Limón, Ph.D.

ven before there was a United States, Hispanics were present in what would become this country. Beginning in the sixteenth century, Spanish explorers traversed North America, and their explorations encouraged settlement as early as the sixteenth century in what is now northern New Mexico and Florida, and as late as the mid-eighteenth century in what is now southern Texas and California.

Later, in the nineteenth century, following Spain's gradual withdrawal from the New World, Mexico in particular established its own distinctive presence in what is now the southwestern part of the United States, a presence reinforced in the first half of the twentieth century by substantial immigration from that country. At the close of the nineteenth century, the U.S. war with Spain brought Cuba and Puerto Rico into an interactive relationship with the United States, the latter in a special political and economic affiliation with the United States even as American power influenced the course of almost every other Latin American country.

The books in this series remind us of these historical origins, even as each explores the present reality of different Hispanic groups. Some of these books explore the contemporary social origins—what social scientists call the "push" factors—behind the excelerating Hispanic immigration to America: political instability, economic underdevelopment and crisis, environmental degradation, impoverished or wholly absent educational systems, and other circumstances contribute to many Latin Americans deciding they will be better off in the United States.

And, for the most part, they will be. The vast majority come to work and work very hard, in order to earn better wages than they would back home. They fill significant labor needs in the U.S. economy and contribute to the economy through lower consumer prices and sales taxes.

When they leave their home countries, many immigrants may initially fear that they are leaving behind vital and important aspects of their home cultures: the Spanish language, kinship ties, food, music, folklore, and the arts. But as these books also make clear, culture is a fluid thing, and these native cultures are not only brought to America, they are also replenished in the United States in fascinating and novel ways. These books further suggest to us that Hispanic groups enhance American culture as a whole.

Our country—especially the young, future leaders who will read these books—can only benefit by the fair and full knowledge these authors provide about the socio-historical origins and contemporary cultural manifestations of America's Hispanic heritage.

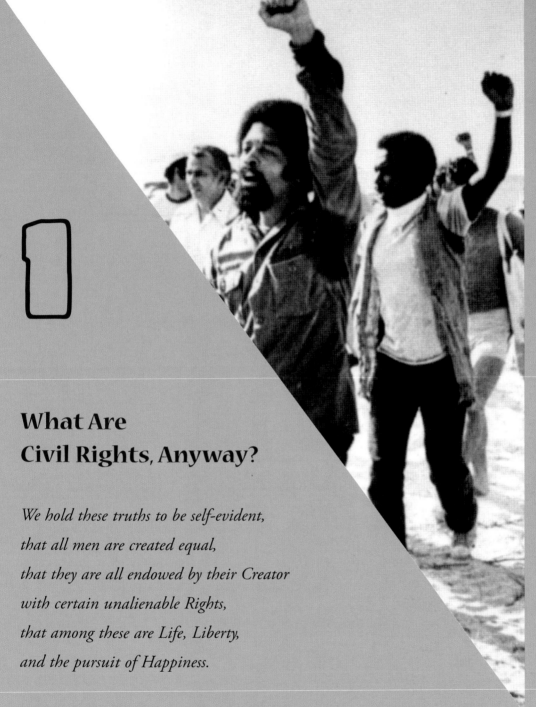

1

What Are Civil Rights, Anyway?

We hold these truths to be self-evident,
that all men are created equal,
that they are all endowed by their Creator
with certain unalienable Rights,
that among these are Life, Liberty,
and the pursuit of Happiness.

—the Declaration of Independence, 1776

Artwork
Details of this mural in Santa Fe, New Mexico, are shown at the beginning of each chapter. The mural depicts the struggle for Latino Civil Rights in the United States.

colonization: the establishment of settlements in another country or place.

"This is Renata Hernandez reporting live in front of the Capitol building for Teledia, where thousands have gathered for a march on Washington to raise awareness of continued discrimination against Hispanic Americans and other minority groups throughout the country. Although the United States Constitution grants a variety of civil rights to its citizens, many Americans believe that some sectors of the population do not get the full benefit of those rights in practice."

The pretty, dark-haired woman continued her report. Behind her, a multitude of men, women, and children walked and danced through the streets, playing music and carrying signs. Many of the people were of Hispanic descent; the crowd was made up of a rainbow of skin colors, from very light to very dark, all gathered together on the beautiful spring day in Washington, D.C. Renata wrapped up her report, promising to continue with her coverage of the story throughout the day.

Renata went back to the Teledia van with her cameraman, who traded his heavy camera for his lighter, more mobile one. She needed to pick up her notepad so she could go interview some of the participants in time for the 6:00 news. She knew that Teledia's largely Hispanic American audience would be very interested in the individual stories of what had brought the protesters here for the day.

he United States of America was formed when colonists became upset with the rule of the British king. The settlers had come to North America looking for opportunity and prosperity. Many gave up homes and livelihoods to sail across the Atlantic Ocean for the chance to be part of the *colonization* of the

Latinos celebrate their identity.

American democracy is based on several documents including the Declaration of Independence.

new land. As time passed and the colonies grew in size, the settlers became more and more dissatisfied with the rule of the king. The people were tired of the lack of rights they endured under British rule, and they fought for change. The British rule was broken in 1776, and a new country was born.

One of the driving forces for America's split from British rule was a lack of personal freedoms and protection from the whims of the ruling class. In the days of the formation of the United States, people had very little say in the decisions of the king. He could declare a plot of land royal property and take it, or he could raise taxes without concern for the taxpayers. One of the most famous lines from the Declaration of Independence states that there will no longer be taxation without representation. The early Americans fought for the right to be heard.

The founders of the United States were remarkable individuals, and they put a staggering amount of planning into the shaping of their new country. And the founders did not only address their own concerns; they also put into the Constitution the Bill of Rights, which has served as the basis for rights that we take for granted every day. The rights we enjoy today were granted by this document produced more than two hundred years ago.

The Bill of Rights consists of the first ten *amendments* to the U.S. Constitution. It grants the American peoples certain freedoms and protections, often called civil rights or civil liberties. These include the freedoms of press, speech, worship, assembly, and the right to bear arms. Because of the Bill of Rights, people cannot be forced to admit to crimes; they can "plead the Fifth" and refuse to tell about their own misdeeds. Americans who are accused of criminal activity are given the protections of due process (preventing the government from simply punishing them without a trial and proper evidence), the right to a trial by jury, and the right to have an attorney assist them through the process. Even someone convicted of a serious crime is safe from cruel and unusual punishment. These rights still flow from the Bill of Rights. In addition, the Constitution has been amended a number of times over the years as different groups won protected rights.

The words quoted from the Declaration of Independence at the start of this chapter have not always been heeded. In spite of the existence of the Bill of Rights and the Constitution, the United States has a long history of discrimination against minorities. Many of the most obvious and remembered abuses were against African

amendments: additions to a legal document.

nly 14 percent of all privately owned businesses in the United States were minority-owned in 2000. Of these, the largest proportion was owned by African Americans.

Americans. Originally, the Bill of Rights was not extended to slaves because they were not considered citizens by law. In fact, the Constitution even acknowledged the existence of slavery in the young United States, stating that each slave would be counted as three-fifths of a person when determining representation in the House of Representatives.

The Civil War was fought, in part, because not everyone in the country agreed about the possession and use of slaves. African Americans, dragged to the country in chains and driven by whips to work their lives away for others, were freed from the toils of slavery. However, the fight to gain basic civil rights was far from over in the mid-1800s when the Emancipation Proclamation freed the slaves. In the twentieth century, Martin Luther King Jr., Malcolm X, Rosa Parks, and others championed the cause of civil rights in their efforts to change the way African Americans

Abraham Lincoln issued the Emancipation Proclamation.

Asian Americans have also faced discrimination.

internment: confinement, imprisonment.

were seen and treated in this country. Unfortunately, African Americans still do not enjoy equal footing with Caucasian (white) Americans in many aspects of everyday life.

During World War II, Japanese Americans' civil rights were also trampled quite thoroughly. As the United States fought a tough war against Germany and Japan, people of Japanese descent throughout the country were rounded up and placed in *internment* camps, supposedly to protect the country from potential spies. The difference in Japanese people's skin color and facial features made them far easier to identify than Germans, and this probably contributed to the willingness of other Americans to suspend their rights. Even American citizens of Japanese ancestry, people

Latino children will be some of tomorrow's leaders.

ispanics are the fastest-growing minority segment in the population at large, and in 2003 became the largest minority group in the United States.

This child deserves the rights and privileges every other American enjoys.

who were born in the United States and had never even set foot on Japanese soil, were put into these camps without a trial. Their rights were brushed aside in the name of national defense.

Hispanic Americans have had similar difficulties in the United States throughout its history. They have often found themselves the target of *discriminatory* practices such as being paid significantly less than white citizens for performing the same task. Although the African American civil rights movement is better known, Hispanic Americans have also had to fight for their constitutionally guaranteed rights. Many scholars believe that the plight of Hispanics in the United States has been as difficult as that of African Americans, but that it is largely ignored by the history books young people study.

Americans whose skin color is even a shade darker than most of the European settlers have a long history of discrimination in the United States. Although *immigrants* settled this country, almost all minorities have had to fight to achieve their rights in the United States. It is difficult to say what drives this prejudice. Perhaps it is cultural misunderstanding or fear of the unfamiliar. The fact remains that discrimination occurs to this day in the United States, regardless of the efforts of many great men and women.

discriminatory: *treating a person or group unfairly because of prejudice about race, ethnicity, age, or gender.*

immigrants: *People who come from one place and settle in another.*

Habla Español

gente (hane-tay): people

mundo (moon-doe): world

lucha (loo-chah): fight

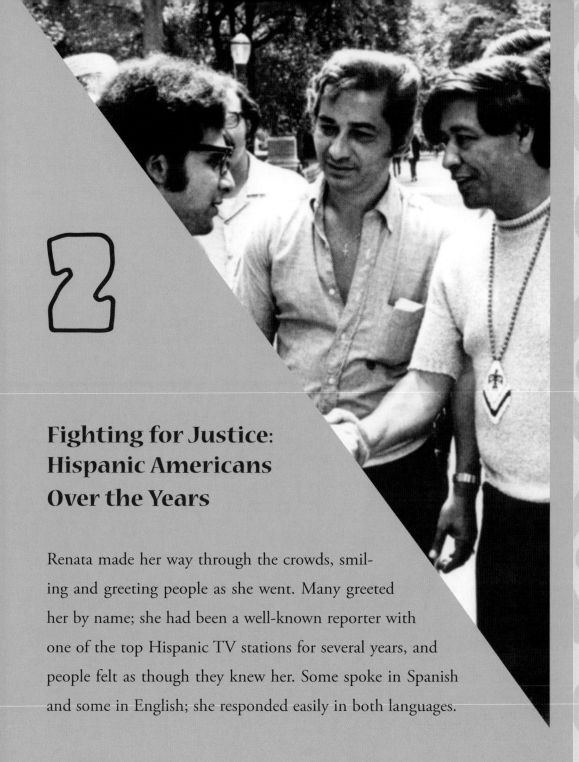

2

Fighting for Justice: Hispanic Americans Over the Years

Renata made her way through the crowds, smiling and greeting people as she went. Many greeted her by name; she had been a well-known reporter with one of the top Hispanic TV stations for several years, and people felt as though they knew her. Some spoke in Spanish and some in English; she responded easily in both languages.

activist: someone who acts in support of a cause.

She glanced at her watch and began to move more purposefully, still smiling at people but moving more quickly. Her producer had scheduled an interview for her with an *activist* from the peak of the Hispanic American civil rights movement.

She saw the man she was looking for talking with several other middle-aged men. His curly salt-and-pepper hair and bushy mustache were a little more neatly trimmed than they would have been in 1970, but he still wore it in the style of many of the Hispanic activists from that era. Renata greeted him and they chatted for a moment before starting the camera rolling.

"This is Renata Hernandez, reporting for Teledia. I'm here today with Juan Gonzalez. Although you may not have heard his name, you have certainly heard the name of his friend and colleague, the great César Chávez."

Renata smiled at Juan and asked him several questions about his background and his work. Juan talked earnestly, explaining his involvement in the civil rights movement during the 1960s and 1970s.

Juan enthusiastically talked about his former colleague, César Chávez. "He was the greatest man I have ever met. We didn't even know we had rights until we met him. We were so proud during that first meeting of the National Farm Workers Association. That day the cause, *La Causa*, was born, and we began to believe that we could someday get fair pay and decent working conditions. He inspired us to be the best we could be!"

lmost everyone living in the United States today is the child, grandchild, great-(or many greats) grandchild of immigrants. The only people who can claim to have truly ancient

César Chávez (second from right) with protest group in New York City

The Hispanic presence adds color throughout the Southwest.

roots on the North American continent are Native Americans. A look back at the family trees of most American citizens will reveal people who came by wagon, boat, car, or plane from someplace else at some point in history.

Interestingly, many Hispanic Americans did not come to the American colonies *after* the formation of the original United States, as did most other ethnic groups. Instead, the *United States* came to a section of the Hispanic American population. Until the mid-1800s, most of southwestern America was Mexican territory, including most of what is now Texas, California, New Mexico, Arizona, Colorado, Nevada, and Utah. In 1848, the

United States gained the land that now forms those seven states under the terms of the Treaty of Guadalupe Hidalgo with Mexico.

The treaty allowed the people in the newly annexed regions to become U.S. citizens immediately if they chose to do so, while keeping their lands. They were Spanish-speaking people who understood little of the prevailing culture of their new country. They did not understand the court system, and greedy people seeking land in the American West took advantage of their lack of knowledge. Settlers came and "won" the land by legal challenges. This is, of course, but one of a long list of discriminations suffered by the Hispanic people in the United States.

our history textbook probably spends much more time talking about the murder of African Americans in the years following the Civil War than about the deaths of Hispanic Americans during the same postwar period. Some people believe this is another instance of American history ignoring the plight of Hispanics. According to the League of United Latin American Citizens, Mexicans as well as African Americans were lynched in the United States between 1865 and 1920.

recruiters: *those people who try to convince people to come to work for someone or to attend a particular school.*

depression: *an economic slump characterized by high unemployment, low production, and poverty.*

repatriation: *sending someone back to the country of his or her birth, or of which he or she is a citizen.*

deportation: *the forcible removal of a foreign national from a country.*

The Beginning of Hispanic Immigration

During the late 1800s and early 1900s, few Hispanic immigrants entered the United States. Later, in the 1920s, as factories and farms of the United States grew beyond the capability of the workforce to fill new jobs, American employers began sending *recruiters* to foreign countries to invite workers to America. There simply were not enough U.S. citizens to perform all the work that was available. This marked the beginning of a massive flow of immigrants from Mexico and Central America. So large was the initial movement that the population of Mexico dropped by one eighth. Nearly two million Mexicans entered the United States looking for work.

The establishment of the first Bracero Program, which was developed as a way to fill low-skill jobs in the United States, allowed thousands of Mexican workers per year to temporarily enter the country. Mexico was suffering a *depression*, and there was widespread poverty and unemployment across the country. The Bracero agreement seemed to benefit both countries, and Mexican workers began entering the United States to find their way out of poverty.

The Mexican immigrants and migrant workers found, however, they were often treated differently than American citizens. They did not enjoy the same wage rates for their work, they had trouble finding housing, and their children were often treated poorly in schools. Many American citizens tended to see Mexican immigrants as invaders taking good work away from

The Bracero Program brought many Latino workers to American farms.

poor Americans. The jobs the immigrants took, however, were ones rarely wanted by American citizens, who thought the work beneath them.

Following the Great Depression, the United States and Mexico developed a new plan to return Mexican workers to their home country. This *repatriation* program led to the *deportation* of nearly 500,000 Mexican Americans. Many Mexican workers were rounded up and held in camps prior to their return to Mexico. According to U.S. immigration law, children born on American soil are automatically granted full citizenship, so the repatriation program broke up many families when workers were deported and their citizen children left behind.

One of the first instances of an organized Hispanic American civil rights movement began with the establishment of the League of United Latin American Citizens (LULAC) in 1927. LULAC formed when three smaller groups decided to band together in Texas to overcome inequality, discrimination, and injustice for Mexican Americans. People who had spent the previous decades struggling just to get by were finally getting the opportunity to look beyond day-to-day survival.

The Great Depression

October 29, 1929, "Black Tuesday," is often cited as the cause of the Great Depression. The stock market crash that occurred that day was just the first highly visible sign of what would become the longest, most severe economic downturn in history.

Migrant workers' children stand beneath the sign for the government's Farm Security Administration in the 1940s.

Many Latinos turned to farmwork during the Depression.

Factories and businesses saw a drastic loss in production and in the sales of goods and services. Many people lost their jobs, and some who were able to keep them found themselves working for a fraction of what they had been paid. Homes were lost because people couldn't pay their mortgages. Banks closed and people lost the money they had saved in them. Many who would never have thought it possible suddenly found themselves relying on charity for food, clothing, and shelter. People stood in line for hours to get a portion of food.

Herbert Hoover was President of the United States when the Great Depression began. He refused to provide government aid to the unemployed. "Hoovervilles," shantytowns of shacks made by the homeless from crates and boxes, could be seen across the country.

Franklin D. Roosevelt defeated Hoover. With the new administration came a series of programs called the New Deal to help counteract the effects of the Depression. Social assistance programs were established that helped people get back on their feet.

Perhaps no group was hurt more by the Depression than the farmers. But economic hardship was not the only crisis they faced. Farmers had been in an economic depression for almost ten years because of low prices for their crops. Prices fell even more with the Great Depression. Then Mother Nature added to the catastrophe with giant dust storms that destroyed many small farms.

Although the Great Depression began in the United States, it quickly spread throughout the industrialized world. In Germany, economic collapse led to the rise to power of Adolf Hitler. Ironically, the Great Depression would not end in the United States until the government began spending large sums of money to support World War II—and defeat Hitler.

Discrimination

ispanic people encountered many barriers to their success in the United States. One large and obvious obstacle was language. The dominant language in the country has always been English, and the Spanish-speaking immigrants were at an immediate disadvantage. Those immigrants who did speak English had a distinct accent that set them apart from others. They did not easily communicate with the English-speaking citizens around them.

ethnic: sharing
cultural traits as a
group.

nativist: someone
who follows a policy
of favoring native
inhabitants.

retention: holding on
to something.

conquistadors:
Spanish conquerors or
adventurers.

Skin color also became a factor in acceptance of the immigrants. Hispanics have found it difficult to blend in with Caucasian Americans. They were not comfortable identifying themselves as a "color" in the way many "white" or "black" individuals did.

Hispanic people are usually much more inclined to retain the behaviors and traditions of their cultures than some other *ethnic* groups. This fact, combined with the difficulties they experienced in becoming part of a community in the United States, played a large part in driving Hispanics to form isolated Spanish-speaking neighborhoods, called *barrios*, in the major ports of entry into the United States. Remaining near to others with similar problems and issues eased the difficult transition to a new country. The isolated communities provided the immigrants some relief from the racist and anti-immigrant (*nativist*) attacks they suffered. The close proximity of their home countries allowed many of the immigrants to maintain contact with their extended families, further strengthening their *retention* of their original culture.

La Raza

hile Hispanic Americans are typically at least partially of Spanish descent, centuries of Spanish rule in Central America and the southern portion of North America led to a mixture of the Spanish and Native populations. While most British settlers of North America viewed Native Americans as inferior people and sought to eradicate them or drive them off,

Hispanic Americans are descended from both Spanish and Native ancestors.

1.
De español é india.
produce mestizo
español 1. india 2. mestizo 3

the Spanish *conquistadors* took a much different approach. The Spaniards' goal was to cause the "savage natives" to convert to a "civilized" culture. They assimilated many of the Native people into their towns and villages, though they did not treat them as equals. Children were born of the new unions, and these children had the traits of both races. Their skin was darker, and they learned Spanish as their primary language. Today, many Hispanic groups speak of this new ethnic group, the descendents of both Spanish and Native people, as a new race—*la Raza* (lah rah-sah).

The descendants of these mixed relationships make up the majority of the people who have come to the United States and form the Hispanic American groups that continue to struggle for their civil rights.

segregation: keeping separate, usually based on race.

The Battle for Civil Liberties

The Hispanic American battle for civil liberties has not been an easy one, and it is certainly not over today. As with other minorities, even the most basic civil rights have not been guaranteed to Hispanic individuals throughout American history.

The beginning of the twentieth century marked the start of the mass immigration of Hispanic people into the United States, yet they remained in the dark ages as far as civil rights are concerned. The many ethnic groups included under the Hispanic umbrella have suffered greatly since the beginning of this mass immigration. Unfortunately, low wages, poor housing, and bad educational outcomes became the normal fare for Hispanic Americans. Although gains have been made, Hispanic Americans continue to earn less money, live in poorer housing, and receive lesser educations than majority Americans.

Many experts consider the end of the 1960s and the beginning of the 1970s to be the golden era of civil rights for a variety of American minority groups, including Hispanic Americans. When people think about civil rights movements, they usually picture African Americans struggling to end unfair practices like *segregation*, with great leaders like Dr. Martin Luther King Jr. speaking to massive crowds. However, almost all minority groups have been subject to discrimination and mistreatment on some level and had to fight for their rights. Some of these movements were far less visible than the African American civil rights movement.

The early Hispanic American civil rights movement received

A civil rights protest in the 1960s

This girl could be considered Quechua, Peruvian, or Hispanic, depending on what classification is being used.

much less attention than that of their African American counterparts for a variety of reasons. The relative lack of media coverage is perhaps the most crucial difference. When stories about discrimination and abuse make it onto mainstream media—television and radio stations and into widely read newspapers and magazines—a large audience can quickly become interested in these problems. This didn't happen with the Hispanic civil rights movement. One possible reason for the lack of media attention could have been because much of the language used throughout the struggle was Spanish. The majority of Americans

uring the 1960s and 1970s, the U.S. government began officially using the term Hispanic to describe people of Spanish descent who spoke Spanish fluently. Many ethnicities, such as Chicanos, Boriquas, and Nuyoricans were grouped together for the purpose of simplification.

• Chicanos are the group of American citizens who gained their citizenship through the Treaty of Guadalupe Hidalgo.
• Boriquas refers to individuals originally from Puerto Rico.
• Nuyoricans are those Puerto Ricans living in New York City.

The U.S. Census Bureau requires that all smaller ethnic groups fitting the description be referred to as Hispanic, including people from twenty-two countries throughout Mexico, South America, and Central America. Many groups saw this change as an insult, but others within the Hispanic community have embraced the term and enjoyed the growing political power associated with membership in a large minority group.

charismatic: having great powers of charm or influence.

could simply not understand. It was far more difficult for mainstream reporters to talk to people involved in the movement, and interviews for television and radio were less appealing, when they had to involve an interpreter. The Hispanic movement also lacked the *charismatic* religious leaders, like Dr. Martin Luther King, who reached out to the American people during the African American civil rights movement. The leaders of the Hispanic American movement were mostly behind the scenes, working silently as organizers. They did not force the struggle into the public eye.

The African American civil rights movement did serve as an inspiration to the increasingly frustrated Hispanic Americans. They were tired of being ignored and mistreated, and they were ready to do something about it. The African American movement also assisted on another critical front: strategy. The leaders of the Hispanic civil rights movement learned a great deal from the efforts of Martin Luther King Jr. and Malcolm X. César Chávez, one of the leaders of the Hispanic civil rights effort, spoke of the influence of Dr. King:

> I learned a lot from him. I was totally in awe of what he did. . . . I was an organizer, so I know what he was going through. . . . I got to know him and we became friends. I began to see. I got involved with some of the things he was doing and also looked to him for advice and guidance.

César Chávez

César Chávez

Chávez was a farmworker tired of the conditions facing Mexican American workers. He led the charge of his farm-worker compatriots in the fight for rights for migrant workers, doing much of his important work during the period of the 1960s and 1970s when so many civil rights activists were working. Chávez was one of the founders of the United Farm Workers, organized to protect the rights of the thousands of workers who were involved in the production of food across the country; this organization remains strong in the United States to this day.

Prior to the efforts of Chávez, farmers tended to see immigrant and migrant farmworkers as just another unlimited asset, much like fertilizer. The workers were often mistreated and underpaid. They were often forced to live and work in deplorable circumstances. These poor conditions caused the workers to strike, refusing to return to work until the situation was addressed. The strike nearly shut down many agricultural sectors because of the heavy reliance of the farmers on cheap labor. But the strikers suffered terrible consequences for their actions. Many times the workers and their families were verbally and physically abused for their efforts. They stayed the course, however, and won their battle. The emergence of the union was a key part in the struggle. By banding together to fight for civil rights, the United Farm Workers became an inspiration for future civil rights activists, both Hispanic and others.

Reies López Tijerina

Reies López Tijerina was another key figure in the struggle for civil rights during the 1960s and 1970s. He became interested in what led to the loss of land by original Mexican Americans who possessed it immediately following the Treaty of Guadalupe Hidalgo. He founded a movement to return the land to the families of those displaced from their lands by the settlers. López Tijerna, unlike most of the other major leaders of the Hispanic American civil rights movement, became increasingly dissatisfied with the more peaceful, legal methods of enacting change. Eventually, he turned to *militancy*, using illegal and violent methods of protest, and spent significant time in prison for his actions.

Habla Español

barrio (bah-ree-oh): neighborhood

trabajador (tra-ba-ha-door): worker

tierra (tee-air-ah): land

Hispanic Civil Rights at Work

As Renata moved away from her interview, she again had time to exchange pleasantries with people as she passed. As she scanned the crowd, a large group of Spanish-speaking families caught her eye. They ranged in age from babies to the elderly, and they were all listening to one man speak. He spoke about fair wages for the workers, about places to live that weren't crowded and dirty, water to drink in the fields, and breaks for the workers. "They cannot do it without you! Without you the fruit would shrivel on the trees! Without you the vegetables would die on the plant! They need you!" He had the group cheering and stamping.

Transportation for migrant workers is often crude or even unsafe.

The young man seemed to be winding down, so Renata decided to wait and see if he would talk to her. After he finished speaking, he went over to a cooler and took out a bottle of water. Renata went over to the young man and introduced herself. He smiled at her, told her that introductions were not necessary, and agreed to talk to her on camera. He explained that he had brought several busloads of migrant workers up from North Carolina for the day.

The young man spoke with passion. "These people came to the United States to fill a need. They take jobs no one else wants. They are here because Americans don't want to harvest apricots or pecans or cucumbers or tobacco or peaches or anything else with the hot sun beating on their backs all day long for a wage that will not feed their families. Look at these people; the lucky ones get paid minimum wage, and many get far less. They live ten or twelve people to a single trailer. Children share beds with their parents or sleep on the floor. In modern America, where some people have five bathrooms in their houses, many of these folks do not have a single working toilet to use. They live in garages, sheds, and even in parking lots. They just want to be able to send money home to their families. They just want to be able to put food in the mouths of their children and clothing on the backs of their loved ones. They pass out in the fields because they haven't been given any water to drink. Sometimes they even die. They get sick from the pesticides that the farmers use. Still they work! Something needs to be done!"

Migrant Workers

boycott: refuse to do or buy something.

he conditions described by the young man are very real, even today. Millions of people across the country, the majority of them of Hispanic descent, move from place to place, working temporary jobs. We call them migrant workers, and most of them work in agriculture, harvesting fruit and vegetable crops, though some work in more industrial settings such as meat-packing plants.

Some of the most significant Hispanic civil rights activity has centered around the rights of migrant workers. César Chávez, called the Father of Hispanic civil rights by some, worked for decades to improve conditions for migrant workers. He started by registering those that were citizens to vote, believing that this would help them to assert political power. By the early 1960s, Chávez was anxious to organize the farmworkers, believing that they would wield far more power if they could present a unified front. He founded an organization called the National Farm Workers Association (NFWA), and they worked to improve conditions for the migrant workers. In 1965, the NFWA became involved in a strike when the grape-growers in California cut the already miserable pay rates. Things dragged on for years with a *boycott* that included as many as 13 million Americans, during which people refused to buy the grapes sold by these growers. Four years later, the growers signed a historic contract with the organization that grew out of the groups that had been involved in the strike. Later, the organization became know as the United Farm Workers.

This button proclaims justice and dignity for farmworkers.

Obviously, battles like these are not won overnight, or even in a decade or two. Chávez continued to work, suffering setbacks and making more victories. His focus and methods changed over the years, but he continued to be a major figure until his death in 1993.

Over the years, laws have been passed that protect migrant workers. Many people believe these laws do not go far enough, and, unfortunately, many employers do not follow the laws. Illegal immigrants especially are at great risk for exploitation because they usually do not dare to complain about poor working conditions for fear of being deported. This issue continues to be at the forefront of Hispanic activism.

Prejudice in the Workplace

espite decades of civil rights movements in the United States, a significant divide between minority groups, particularly those of color, and Americans of Eastern European descent remains. More European Americans hold middle- to high-paid positions than any other ethnic group. In general, the jobs available for minorities are low-paying, low-skill service or industry (factory) positions. The divide tends to promote further discrimination in employment, in part because poverty breeds poor educational outcomes. It can be very difficult for the child of a poor family to gain admittance to colleges and universities, continuing the cycle of poverty.

Franklin Roosevelt

American employers have a long history of discrimination against Hispanic Americans. One of the first offenses that gained public attention was the unequal access to government jobs suffered at the time of World War II. Qualified workers were passed over for well-paid government work simply because of the color of their skin. Following many public displays, the various groups fighting for civil rights caught the attention of President Franklin Roosevelt, who issued an Executive Order forbidding discrimination by defense industries and contractors against workers. He created a special commission known as the Federal Employment Practices Commission to police the industries and guard against further discrimination. The war raged on overseas, and Hispanic Americans were fighting and dying for the country, yet they were being denied equal access to the jobs that would help them out of poverty.

The same Latina woman who received a Bronze Medal after her son was killed in the Korean War also faced discrimination from other Americans.

Spreading Discrimination

As World War II was ending, discrimination in the workplace was actually growing. The armed forces were sending the soldiers home, and they were eager to return to work. White males received preference for nearly every position. The G.I. Bill was passed to help the men who had served in the military enter college and purchase homes. At the same time, many Hispanic American individuals were denied admittance to colleges due in part to their poor educations, but also because they were Hispanic Americans. The housing market was booming, yet Hispanic Americans were denied loans that would have been used to purchase houses in primarily white neighborhoods.

As discrimination continued and expanded beyond the workplace, the general public began to take notice. Court decisions such as *Brown v. Board of Education* (1954) began chipping away at discriminatory practices throughout the country. Lawmakers and Presidents began acting to put an end to the poor treatment of minorities.

equal access: *removal of barriers, which may be physical and/or attitudinal, to provide access to a building, a facility, or to use of a program, product, or service, and give all people the same quality of use, benefit, and opportunity.*

Affirmative Action

n 1961, President John F. Kennedy issued an Executive Order requiring all federal contractors to treat all applicants equally regardless of race, color, religion, sex, or national origin. An oversight commission was proposed as part of President Kennedy's civil rights legislation sent to Congress in 1963. The commission would develop methods for ensuring *equal access* for all people and to monitor the federal contractors.

President Lyndon Johnson signed the Civil Rights Act of 1964 (which took effect one year later), which prohibited discrimination by employers with more than fifteen employees. The Equal Employment Opportunity Commission (EEOC) was established under the new law. President Johnson issued an Executive Order shortly after the passage of the Civil Rights Act that required all government contractors and subcontractors to create more job opportunities for minorities. He also created a governmental office within the Department of Labor to assess whether the contractors were complying with the terms of the law and his Executive Order. He later amended the Executive Order to include women of all ethnic origins.

President Richard Nixon joined in the action soon after he was sworn into office. In 1969, he issued an Executive Order that set flexible goals and timetables designed to help correct what he called "under-utilization of minorities" by federal contractors. He also issued an Executive Order that set forth plans and programs for a National Minority Business Enterprise Constructing Program to help minorities start up businesses.

The majority of these actions included colleges and universities because of the amount of federal funding granted to them each year. Many lawmakers realized that equal opportunity in education was critical to equality in other aspects of society.

Of course, some in America opposed the governmental efforts to promote equality. Demonstrations against the adoption of *affirmative action* policies sprang up in communities across the country. The 1960s, however, were a time of plenty in the United States. Unemployment rates were very low, and the economy was growing fast. Employers found that they needed to hire minority workers if they intended to keep growing; there were not enough employees to do otherwise. The United States was involved in yet another war, and many minority soldiers were dying in Vietnam for their country.

Times quickly changed in the early 1970s when a nationwide *recession* set in. Jobs that were plentiful in the 1960s dried up and poverty grew sharply. Middle-class families found that they could no longer survive on one income, marking a fundamental change in the family structure. Families, once able to thrive with one parent working and the other staying home to raise the children, found they needed two working parents. This change caused even greater pressure on the job market.

One effect the recession had on minorities was a severe increase in discrimination and prejudice in the workplace. Employers again started hiring white men over minorities. The progress made during the 1960s began to fade. Unemployed European Americans began to see employed minority workers, particularly Hispanic American and African American individuals, as a threat to the "American Dream." Pressure began to build to reverse the affirmative action policies instituted during the previous decade of civil rights advances. Politicians, always fearful for their jobs, took notice.

Richard Nixon, who helped establish the policies and goals of affirmative action, began to backtrack. His *federal-court nominees* had records of speaking against affirmative action. Presidents Gerald Ford, Ronald Reagan, and George H. W. Bush each followed his lead and appointed justices that acted to weaken affirmative action and equal opportunity.

In the 1980s, the average Hispanic household income level remained far lower than that of European American families. Hispanic families had an average income of just $20,306 per year. When this figure is compared to the average income of European Americans ($32,274 per year), it becomes clear that the efforts of the civil rights movements of the past were insufficient. According to the U.S. Census Bureau, in 1987, 23.4 percent of all Hispanic households were below the poverty level; only 8.2 percent of European American families were impoverished. Hispanic Americans also had a much greater rate of unemployment during the 1980s than any ethnic group other than African Americans. About five percent of European Americans willing and able to work were unemployed compared to nearly nine percent of Hispanic Americans. These differences in income were largely due to discrimination against Hispanic Americans in the workplace and lower overall educational levels.

Several independent studies revealed that affirmative action, while forcing employers to hire and pay minority workers wages similar to nonminority employees, failed to cause an increase in upper-level opportunities within companies. European Americans were twice as likely to be promoted to a managerial or professional position as Hispanic Americans. European Americans were also far more likely be given substantial raises in pay.

affirmative action: *a program designed to increase the employment opportunities of certain groups.*

recession: *A downturn in economic activity on a large scale.*

federal-court nominees: *individuals who are nominated by the President to serve as judges in federal courts.*

ésar Chávez is probably the best known Hispanic American civil rights organizer ever. He developed his passion for improving the lives of migrant workers through experience. Chávez was born into a family of farmers in Arizona before the start of the Great Depression. When he was ten years old, his family lost their farm and had to join the ranks of migrant workers who followed the crops in California. He was forced to live in dirty, crowded homes, with no electricity or running water, moving from place to place as different crops came into season. They had to move so often that Chávez and his siblings were forced to attend more than thirty different schools. In spite of frequent moves, uncaring teachers, part-time field work, and discrimination against Spanish-speakers, Chávez graduated from the eighth grade, quite a feat for a migrant worker in the 1940s.

César Chávez

omen have been involved in the Hispanic American civil rights movement. Dolores Huerta was born in New Mexico in 1930. She became involved in a community group supporting farmworkers when she met César Chávez and helped him form the National Farm Workers Association, which eventually became the United Farm Workers (UFW). She was very active in the early years of the farmworkers' organization and was one of the key figures in a widespread grape boycott that helped the UFW become nationally recognized.

Huerta's civil rights victories were not limited to the UFW. In 1988, while demonstrating peacefully against the policies of presidential candidate George H. W. Bush, she was severely injured when police clubbed the demonstrators. She eventually won a considerable financial settlement from the police, as well as changes in police policy on handling demonstrations.

osé Angel Gutiérrez is one of the recognized leaders of the Chicano movement in the United States. He was a critical figure in the civil rights movement for all Hispanic citizens, but one of the things he is best known for is a book he wrote, *A Gringo Manual on How to Handle Mexicans*. He wrote the book to educate the leaders of grassroots political movements about good strategies for organizing people and negotiation.

Habla Español

uvas (ooh-vahs): grapes

presidente (prays-ee-dane-tay): president

mujeres (moo-hair-ase): women

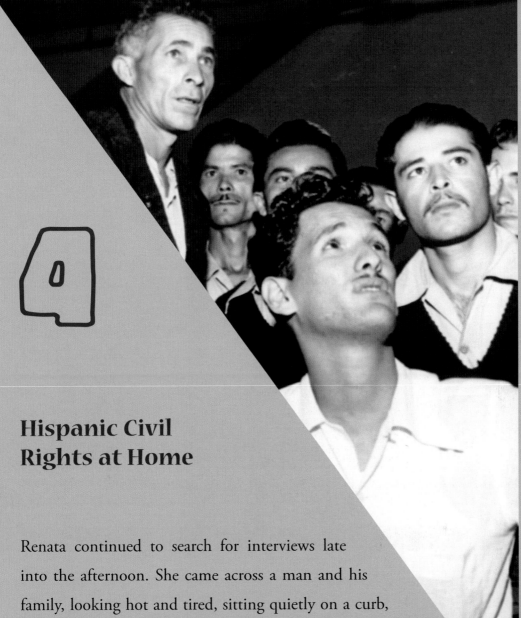

Hispanic Civil Rights at Home

Renata continued to search for interviews late into the afternoon. She came across a man and his family, looking hot and tired, sitting quietly on a curb, and holding up a sign that said "Unfair Housing Hurts My Children!" She approached the man, introduced herself, and told him of her purpose for being there that day.

"I know you," he said with a smile "I watch Teledia every day after work. My name is Pedro Figueroa." Renata smiled at him and asked if he would be willing to share his story with the world.

Latinos have lived in the Southwest longer than Anglos, intermingling with Native people.

"Yes, if you think it will help," the man replied. Renata smiled and called her cameraman over. The man stood and faced the camera, less than confident in his big television debut. He tried in vain to smooth his shirt and fix his hair, which were mussed from the heat and wind, but gave up after Renata assured him it would not matter. She knew that his story was more powerful if he looked like the events had been hard for him to handle; pictures were often more valuable than words. Renata talked with Pedro for a few minutes to calm his nerves and to discuss what brought him to the rally and then began to film.

"This is Renata Hernandez, reporting for Teledia. I'm here today with Pedro Figueroa and his family. Pedro hails from southern California. He owns a chain of business supply stores that operates in many urban areas of the Southwest."

She turned to Pedro and he began to tell his story. Pedro told her of the struggles his family had been through in their attempts to purchase a home in a suburban neighborhood. He told of real estate agents only showing him homes in minority neighborhoods, even though they were well below the price range he had specified. He told of fighting to even look at the homes he wanted to buy in the neighborhoods where he wanted to raise his children. He had placed several offers on homes, good offers, only to be turned down each time. After a long, fruitless search, Pedro began to think about bringing a lawsuit. Finding an attorney wasn't easy, but he eventually found one that was interested in helping him.

"We are going to file suit soon, and we are hoping to make a difference. However, in the meantime we are still living in a cramped apartment, and my children are still going to the same, poor school. We are so tired!"

The Expanding United States

In the United States, the availability of safe, clean, and affordable housing is considered by most to be a basic human right. A portion of the "American Dream" has always been home ownership. Many people originally came to the country to carve out a space to call their own. Land was plentiful and easily accessible in the formative years of the country. Over the decades, the population of the United States grew and the amount of available space decreased. As land became more and more scarce, discrimination against minorities increased across the country.

A great westward migration of settlers seeking land marked the beginning of the mistreatment of Hispanic American home- and landowners. Most lost the lands that their families had tended for years to the wave of European American settlers rushing to the West. Although they were technically U.S. citizens according to the terms of the Treaty of Guadalupe Hidalgo, most Hispanic American families living on the lands acquired by the United States at the end of the Mexican-American War were driven out in much the same way as Native Americans were from their ancestral lands. Manifest Destiny was the belief that Americans had a God-given right to expand the country's borders as far as they could, and they chased this goal ruthlessly. There were few barriers to the expansion. The court system was often called on to decide land ownership questions, and Hispanic Americans, not able to speak English well enough to defend themselves or to understand the way the system worked, usually lost. Their lands were taken from them and given to the white settlers.

Landless

The years following the westward expansion of European Americans were not kind to Hispanic Americans. Without their lands, they were forced to live on lands owned by others. The typical arrangement involved a work-for-housing arrangement. The European American settlers allowed the Hispanic Americans to live on their lands so long as they worked the farms. Pay for the work was extremely poor. Often, families earned barely enough money to survive. Typically, Hispanic American families chose to live near one another in relatively isolated barrio communities in order to support one another in a traditional fashion. The formation of the barrios allowed Hispanic American families to resist the pressure to blend in with the predominantly white communities. One result of this was the maintenance of cultural traditions and the persistence of Spanish as the pri-

Latinos protest rent increases in New York City.

mary language, which tended to increase discrimination by the European Americans. The abuses gradually increased over the years until they gained enough notice to be addressed by law.

According to the current laws of the United States, all families, regardless of race, religion, or political affiliation have the right to own a proper home should they choose to do so. In many areas of the country, home-ownership opportunities are few and far between for Hispanic American families. Often, these families face difficulties in finding or buying homes other ethnic groups do not.

class-action lawsuit has been filed against Fannie Mae, a mortgage company that was created to expand minority home ownership, alleging that the company's new computerized system of deciding which loans to finance discriminates against minorities. The lawsuit claims that using a system that analyzes people only in terms of numbers puts Hispanics and African Americans at a disadvantage.

The Civil Rights Act

According to the magazine *People en Español*, 46 percent of Hispanics owned a home in 2001, up seven percent from 1991.

s with other basic civil rights, it took the intervention of the government to set the table for change. In 1968, the U.S. government passed a law called the Civil Rights Act, which set forth basic protections to civil rights for all Americans. One part of the law established guidelines specific to the process of buying or selling a home. Under the rules of the law, no person or family can be denied the opportunity to purchase or rent a home based on their ethnic background. The law

Latino strikers for better wages

requires the seller of the home, real estate agent, insurance companies, and mortgage companies to treat each prospective homebuyer equally.

A common practice prior to the passage of the law was the establishment of different loan terms for minorities than for European Americans. The costs of taking out a mortgage were significantly higher for minority families. The practice came to be known as predatory lending, because banks would lure prospective buyers with low advertised loan rates and fees, then switch to the higher "minority" rates. The banks made a much greater profit from these loans. Home sellers and landlords would refuse to give equal consideration to otherwise equally qualified applicants because of the color of their skin. Hispanic American and African American families were often denied the opportunity to purchase or rent homes in predominantly white neighborhoods.

The passage of this Civil Rights Act was intended to reduce the discrimination suffered by minorities. Unfortunately, there are regions of the country where the law is largely ignored even today. Hispanic Americans and African Americans are discriminated against more than any other ethnic groups when it comes to housing. According to a report by the Center for Community Change, certain minority groups are still heavily discriminated against across the country. Hispanic Americans, African Americans, Native Americans, and Asian Americans are far less able to purchase homes at the lowest interest rates. Hispanic Americans are far more likely to be denied when they apply for a rental property or when they apply for mortgages.

Searching for Solutions

he slow increase in home prices over the years has also had an effect on the ability of Hispanic Americans to purchase homes. In California, the average price of a new home recently rose above $220,000. Less than 30 percent of all Hispanic American families in California could afford a home at those prices, compared to nearly 40 percent of European American families who could find it within their means. There are very few affordable housing opportunities for minorities throughout the country in desirable locations. Typically, housing for lower-income Americans is found in inner-city neighborhoods frequently associated with high crime rates and joblessness.

Overall, housing discrimination is on the decline, but it decreased less for Hispanic Americans than for any other ethnic group between 1989 and 2000, according to a U.S. Housing and Urban Development (HUD) study. The study compared the experiences of test "families" of varying ethnic backgrounds in twenty major housing markets. Each test family had the same exact work history, financial history, and references. Hispanic American testers were discriminated against 25 percent of the time when applying for a rental property and 20 percent of the time when the intent was to buy the home, the highest rate of any ethnicity in the study. Hispanic Americans were far less likely than any of the groups to receive information about the properties or be invited to visit the home.

The unequal footing of minority families in the national housing market has not gone unnoticed by the federal government. Home ownership opens many doors for families. Owners start to build equity from the moment they make their first payment, and they are able to use the home as collateral for loans that can improve the quality of life. The housing industry is a major part of the U.S. economy, and when people are able to purchase homes, the economy grows. It is not surprising that politicians have taken notice of the situation.

The average household income for Hispanics increased from $14,712 in 1980 to $29,500 in 1996 and is currently at $33,980—a 132 percent increase.

According to the Latin Business Association, in the last two decades, the number of Hispanic-owned businesses in the Southland has grown three times faster than the Hispanic population; there are now over 500,000 Hispanic-owned businesses in California.

Habla Español

banco (bon-koe): bank

casa (cah-sah): house

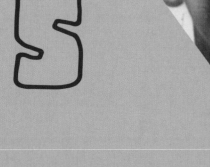

5

Hispanic Civil Rights and Politics

After Renata said adios to the Figueroa family, she decided it was time to check her messages on her cell phone. She had gotten so caught up in the stories that she had neglected that obligation. Renata discovered a message from her producer saying they had set up another interview for her with a representative from a nearby state who had come to the rally to show his support for the participants. She gathered her things and headed back to her van, where she would be meeting the gentleman in a few minutes.

A man in a traditional suit and tie was waiting not so patiently for her at the van when she arrived. Renata was exhausted from her long day in the crowd, but she put a smile on her face and greeted him. As a veteran of many TV interviews, Miguel did not need the same time to relax as Pedro had required. Miguel smiled for the camera and launched into his story. He was here today to promote voter registration and involvement in the political process.

Miguel explained, "The best and truly the only way that we can improve the lives of Hispanic Americans across the United States is by getting involved. As the fastest-growing ethnic group in this country, Hispanics can exercise great political power if they will just step up to the plate and get involved. Voting is the best thing you can do for yourself and for your country."

The young reporter heartily agreed with his sentiment, having worked for a voter registration campaign herself over the years. She was glad to add him to her list of interviews for the day. After she finished her wrap up, she thanked him for his time and sent him on his way. He had been much more pleasant than she had expected a politician to be.

The Path to Equality

The path to equality in a democracy passes through the political system. In order for any group to achieve true equality, they must have political representation. At present, there are more than thirty-seven million Hispanic American citizens living in the United States, and the population is growing at a faster rate than any other ethnic group; 13.3 percent of the country's population is of Hispanic origin. Presidential candidates have long realized the power of the Hispanic American vote, and they spend great amounts of money to impress this quickly growing ethnic group. The rapid growth of the Hispanic American population has led to a slight increase in their political power, but representation in government remains extremely low compared to the population. In order to be truly equal, Hispanic Americans must be equally represented in government.

Hispanic Americans started to become active participants in politics during the early 1960s when they began their fight for civil rights. The people realized that they needed greater political representation to continue their quest for empowerment. Though laws such as the Civil Rights Act of 1964 and the Voting Rights Act of 1965 opened the door for greater political participation for many minorities, Hispanic Americans remain among the least politically represented ethnic groups in the country. In 2000, there were over 500,000 elected officials in the United States. Fewer than 5,000, less than one percent, of those positions were held by Hispanic Americans. Congress has the highest percentage of Hispanic Americans of any elected federal government post. In the House of Representatives there are 435 seats. However, Hispanic Americans held only twenty-five seats, which is equal to about six percent of the total. It is obvious that there is not equality in government for Hispanic Americans, a fact that affects the ability of Hispanic Americans to change laws and policies that affect them as a group.

Several factors affect the Hispanic American political movement. According to a U.S. Census Bureau survey, only 12.5 percent of all Hispanic Americans eligible to vote did so in the 2000 presidential election. Across the country, there is very low participation in voting among people of all ethnicity between the ages of eighteen and twenty-five. The average age of the Hispanic American population in 2000 was 25.5 years of age. Voting participation is even lower within some of the groups that make up the Hispanic American population. Mexican Americans, for example, average about twenty years of age, while Puerto Rican Americans average about twenty-one. The group with the highest percentage of political participation among Hispanic Americans is the Cuban Americans, whose average age is approximately thirty-five. Another important factor in the low voter turnout of Hispanic Americans is that a large number of them are legal U.S. residents who do not yet have voting rights. According to a study of the 1998 presidential election, 52 percent of Hispanic Americans legally in the United States were not allowed to vote because of voter registration rules. A third key factor in the low voter turnout among Hispanic Americans is poverty. Impoverished individuals are far less likely to vote than middle-class individuals even though they have more to gain from strong participation. Low educational levels, lack of trust in the political system, and even an inability to get to polling places are key aspects of the

bilingual: *knowing or using two languages.*

conservative: *resistant to change.*

liberal: *a person who favors a political philosophy of progress and reform and the protection of civil liberties.*

In 2004, there were a record number of Hispanics serving in government. Twenty-five Hispanics were members of the 108th Congress. All served in the House, and one was a delegate; twenty were Democrats, seven were women. Two Hispanic members were brothers (Mario and Lincoln Diaz-Balart, Republicans from Florida), and two were sisters (Linda and Loretta Sanchez, Democrats from California).

low turnout among impoverished people. More Hispanic Americans live below the poverty level than any other ethnic group in the country.

While Hispanic Americans represent a large and rapidly growing group of people within the United States, it may be difficult for them to unify in a way that increases their political power. Grouped under the term "Hispanic American" are people from twenty-two different nations. Each nationality has different cultures and traditions. Some Hispanic Americans speak primarily Spanish, some are *bilingual*, and still others speak English as their primary language. The religions worshipped cover a very broad spectrum, including Catholic, Protestant, Jewish, Buddhist, and several others. Many of the nationalities contained within the Hispanic American group have been present in the country for several generations, while others have newly entered the country. The reasons for entering the United States are just as varied. Some immigrants came for jobs and economic opportunity while others came to escape political unrest. These differences all play a role in preventing Hispanic Americans from coming together to exert their full political influence in the country.

The many nationalities entering the United States over the years became concentrated in different areas of the country. Mexican Americans, for example, primarily settled in the southwestern part of the country, in the regions granted to the United States by the Treaty of Guadalupe Hidalgo. The majority of Cuban Americans settled in southern Florida. Puerto Rican Americans concentrated in the northeastern United States, mainly New York City. In these regions, Hispanic American groups have had some political success. In the years following World War II, however, Hispanic American groups historically centered in certain regions of the country began to spread to

Miami, Florida, has many Latino communities.

other areas. As the different nationalities have spread out, they have begun to find that their political impact is lessened due to the decreased local population. To combat this, the groups have attempted to form alliances with other Hispanic American groups of different nationalities to increase their political power. The difficulties of this approach soon became apparent. The various nationalities have very different political goals. Cuban Americans, for example, are traditionally *conservative* and tend to vote for Republican candidates, while Mexican Americans are *liberal* and tend to vote Democratic.

Some issues are important to the majority of Hispanic Americans regardless of their nation of origin. Many pieces of legislation have served as unifying points for the diverse groups of Hispanic Americans in the United States. For the most part, Hispanic

The immigration building in Miami, Florida

Americans support any legislation that increases assistance for families and education. Culturally, Hispanic Americans place greater value on family than almost any other ethnic group. Any legislation that will improve the quality of life for their families is greeted with open arms. Programs that support the use of bilingual education are also very popular among Hispanic American voters. They are highly aware of the problems that Hispanic American youths face in schools across the country. Many feel that promoting bilingual education will help decrease school drop-out rates among Spanish-speaking Hispanic American students.

Reforming Immigration

air immigration reform laws are another key point that many Hispanic Americans are interested in supporting. When the Immigration Reform and Control Act (IRCA) of 1986 passed, Hispanic Americans were divided over the benefits and costs of the law. Many argued that certain parts of the law were poorly written. They believed that the section that imposed fines on employers who hired illegal immigrants might increase workplace discrimination against all Hispanic individuals. In a study three years after passage of the IRCA, the General Accounting Office found that discrimination against Hispanic Americans had indeed increased. Many employers refused to hire Hispanics out of fear that they might be illegal immigrants with forged paperwork.

Immigration reform remains one of the most hotly contested topics among Hispanic Americans year to year. It is a heavily debated issue in every election year as politicians

ispanic individuals holding important offices often have more power than anyone else to advance the cause of civil rights. The Honorable Joseph Marion Hernandez of Florida was the first Hispanic to serve in the U.S. House of Representatives. Although Hispanic Americans have not historically had great political power, Hernandez held that position more than 180 years ago.

suggest new policies to reduce the number of illegal immigrants entering the country each year. Illegal immigrants are a sure bet for getting the attention of the American people, and the Hispanic American community as a whole is at the center of the debate.

The Language Question

relatively new area of concern for Hispanic Americans is a movement toward the establishment of English as the official language of government. Several lawmakers have proposed legislation that would outlaw the use of any language other than English by the federal government. None of the pieces of legislation have been adopted into law, but the pressure remains. In 1996, for example, the House of Representatives passed a resolution that would have made English the official language of the U.S. government, but it was defeated in the Senate. Several states have passed laws establishing English as the official language. The danger of an English-only policy is that it weakens support for bilingual education and public programs. Sooner or later, court challenges could weaken or put an end to publicly funded bilingual programs.

r. Hector P. García, an immigrant from Tamaulipas, Mexico, was an important figure in the Hispanic American civil rights movement. He rallied Mexican American war veterans into a very effective and powerful lobby group after becoming aware of one particular incident in which a funeral home in Texas refused to bury a Mexican soldier because of his ethnic origin. Garcia's civil rights organization, the American G.I. Forum, was instrumental in helping President John F. Kennedy become the first Catholic President of the United States. The influence of this group has affected both elections and policy over the years.

Habla Español

derecho (day-ray-cho): right

gobierna (go-bee-air-na): government

Hispanic Civil Rights and Education

Renata knew her producers would appreciate
one or two more interviews so that they could do a
lengthy segment with the 6:00 news. Her feet hurt,
and she was hot and tired, but she was a professional. She
put on her game face and ventured back out.

The face of the future

A group of children with signs saying things like "We are the future! Teach us!" and "Education is the best investment!" caught Renata's eye. She knew that both her producers and the public loved the cute faces of young children. Renata hurried over to the group to make their acquaintance. Her familiar face usually helped her in these situations. Plus, almost everyone here today would appreciate the opportunity to tell their stories to a wider audience.

She quickly learned that the group of children, teachers, and parents had come from a largely Hispanic neighborhood school to raise awareness of the continued problems in the educational system for Hispanic American children. Renata got permission from one parent to talk with her daughter, a dark-eyed girl of about eight or nine years named Marisol.

Not surprisingly, Marisol was a little shy at first, but she warmed up to Renata quickly. The child told Renata about her school. "Our teacher is really nice. She brings us in treats every Friday. There aren't enough desks for everybody, but we take turns. I sometimes wish that the windows weren't boarded up, but at least we get to go outside for recess almost every day."

Marisol's teacher shared more information about the school's situation. They had been forced to lay off a number of teachers because of budget cuts and were no longer able to provide the sorts of services that they had at one point for children who spoke no English. Children were falling behind and failing the state's mandatory tests. "We want people to know that the days of segregation and 'separate but equal' may be over, but our children are still getting the short end of the stick. We cannot get ahead if we do not educate our children!"

The Value of Education

Education is one of the most important aspects of life for all people. Well-educated citizens are better able to provide for themselves and their families, and are better able to raise and educate their own children. Well-educated people are better equipped to work managerial or high-skilled positions, earn higher salaries with better benefits, and stay employed for long periods of time. Unemployment rates in the United States are twice as high for workers without a high school diploma than for those holding one. The work that is to be found in the country is changing. As many as 80 percent of all jobs in the United States now require thinking rather than physical skills; in the past, the majority of work was of a low-skill physical nature. It has been estimated that approximately 52 percent of available jobs in the United States will now require some form of postsecondary education. Increasing education has been shown to have a direct positive impact on savings, investments, earnings, and employment.

Hispanic Americans are among the least educated of all ethnic groups. Nearly 35 per-

GED: *General Equivalency Degree obtained by successful completion of a test; substitutes for a high school diploma.*

cent of all employed Hispanic Americans do not hold a high school diploma or *GED*, compared to 13 percent for workers of non-Hispanic origin. Only about 10 percent of Hispanic American employees hold managerial or professional positions, while about 25 percent of non-Hispanics do. These higher-paid positions require a higher degree of education, and many Hispanic Americans find themselves unqualified for them. Until the educational outcomes of Hispanic Americans are improved, it will be difficult for them to have and keep these jobs.

Hispanic Americans have made gains in education over the past decade but remain significantly less well educated than European or African Americans at all grade levels. Over that same time period, the number of Hispanic American students in U.S. schools has grown at a rate faster than any other ethnic group. In fact, the number of European American students has actually decreased.

The Earlier the Better

Early childhood education is an effective tool in promoting educational achievement. Hispanic American children are far less likely to be enrolled in pre-kindergarten educational programs than European American or African American children. Only one out of every five Hispanic American three-year-olds was enrolled in early education programs in 2000. At the same time, two out of every five European American three-year-olds were. This difference is partially due to increased social awareness of the existence and usefulness of such programs. In

According to the U.S. Department of Education, Hispanic students continue to struggle with higher education, scoring an average of 9 percent to 11 percent lower than white students on standardized college-admission tests. While only a tenth of white freshmen need remedial English classes when they enter college, a quarter of Hispanic students are asked to take them. The majority of Hispanic students are asked to take remedial mathematics courses, as compared to only a third of white freshmen. Hispanic students' college grades tend to be lower, and they often end up taking longer to get their degrees.

primarily European American neighborhoods, enrolling a child in an early education program is common. Hispanic American children are typically kept home and educated in a way that is more in keeping with the traditional methods. The number of Hispanic American children enrolled in programs for four-year-olds is much higher but still significantly below that of European American children. Approximately half of all Hispanic American four-year-olds are enrolled in these programs, while nearly 75 percent of all European American four-year-olds are. School enrollment at kindergarten age is actually slightly higher for Hispanic American than European American children.

Throughout the elementary school years, Hispanic American children are far less likely to be enrolled in gifted and talented programs than European American students. In the general school population, Hispanic American students accounted for approxi-

Hispanic students are more likely to repeat grades.

mately 13 percent of all students enrolled in U.S. schools but only about six percent of the gifted and talented population. By comparison, 65 percent of all students and about 80 percent of all gifted and talented students were European American. Hispanic American students are far more likely to be "held back" at a grade level than European American students. They are also far more likely to drop out of school than any other ethnic group. In 1997, only about 70 percent of Hispanic American students completed high school.

The poor educational performance of Hispanic American students in high school directly affects their ability and desire to enter college. In 1996, only one-third of all Hispanic American students who had completed high school chose to enroll in college immediately after graduation. This figure has risen slightly, but there is still a large difference between the enrollment of Hispanic American and European American students in colleges and universities across the country.

One of the most noticeable differences between the education of the majority of Hispanic Americans and European Americans is the makeup of the schools. Many of the schools attended by Hispanic American students are essentially segregated. Few European American students attend these schools. The majority of Hispanic American families in the United States live in poor city neighborhoods and are unable to afford to send their children to better schools in the suburbs. There has been a decline in the exposure of Hispanic American students to European American students, resulting in a decline in understanding and acceptance between the two groups.

Latino teens often don't have as many opportunities as Anglos.

Assembly at a Latino school

The Language Barrier

ublic policy has done little to improve the education of Hispanic American youths. The fact that many speak Spanish as their primary language has served as a barrier to education for many years. In addition, the passage of laws banning the use of bilingual education has been a serious setback to the education of Hispanic American students. On June 2, 1998, English-only *advocates* in California struck a major blow to proponents of

advocates: people who plead for a cause or propound an idea.

ispanic children in the late 1800s and the first half of the 1900s often had worse situations than African American students. Because segregation required that African American school systems be "separate but equal," some thought was given to funding those programs. Of course, African American programs were nowhere near equal, but at least they were guaranteed some funding. Because Hispanic children were considered white by the law, there was no formalized system for separate schools. However, the European American school system did not wish to school "white" children with Hispanics, so separate schools did exist. These schools often did not have any clubs or sports teams because there was no funding offered for such things.

ballot initiative: A
public policy question
decided by a vote of
the people.

integrating students' cultural background into education with the passage of California's Proposition 227. This *ballot initiative*, passed by an overwhelming majority and, some say, fueled by the growing anti-immigrant sentiment in the state, put an end to California's system of bilingual education. California's non-Hispanic white majority approached minority status for the first time (only 53 percent in 1998, according to the California Department of Finance) when this initiative was introduced, and some experts believe that Proposition 227 passed because the slim white majority, who composed a very large percentage of the voting population, felt that their very way of life was threatened.

Proposition 227 amended California's Education Code to require that "all children in California public schools shall be taught English by being taught in English." Under this law, children whose native language is not English receive temporary services to help them transition for a period of no more than a year and then must be placed in English language classrooms. The law provides for limited exceptions, and is written to ensure they are not often used.

The issue of bilingual education in California is further complicated by the existence of the Treaty of Guadalupe Hidalgo, which was signed in 1848 when the United States annexed a portion of Mexico, the territory that became the Southwest United States, including states like California and Arizona. Many advocates of bilingual education interpret this treaty as guaranteeing the people who were living in the territory at the time the treaty was signed the right to continue their language and culture without interference from the U.S. government.

A variety of organizations, including the America Civil Liberties Union (ACLU) and several minority legal groups, chal-

A protest march in New York City for educational rights

Children like this will grow up speaking two languages.

lenged the legality of Proposition 227 immediately following its passage and tried to keep it from going into effect. They argued that the law was inconsistent with federal education law, that it discriminated against people on the basis of their *national origin*, and that it violated the Constitution. Nevertheless, the courts allowed the law to take effect. Although additional challenges to the law have occurred over the years since its passage, it has been upheld by state and federal courts.

national origin: the country of one's birth.

Habla Español

numéro (noo-mare-oh): number

educación (aid-oo-ca-see-own): education

oney seems to be a factor in Hispanic Americans poorer educational outcomes. In addition to funding problems in school systems in Hispanic neighborhoods and the decrease in funding for bilingual education programs, Hispanic American students have more trouble paying for their education after high school. Only about a fifth of white college freshman have major concerns about how to pay for their education, but more than three-quarters of incoming Hispanic college students are very concerned about how to finance their education. One reason for this is that Hispanic students often do not take full advantage of the financial aid that is available, particularly loans, which usually account for most of the available assistance. This may occur because Hispanic parents are less likely to have gone to college themselves and may not be aware of the options.

hen most people think of segregation in schools, they think of African Americans in their own separate schools. However, segregation was not limited to African Americans. Mexican Americans and other Hispanics throughout the Southwest were forced to do all of their learning in separate and clearly inferior facilities during the first half of the twentieth century. Fortunately, Hispanic Americans, like other minorities, did not all quietly accept this. The court system provided one good way to fight against injustice. Mexican Americans won several victories that weakened separation. These cases included *Delgado v. Bastrop ISD*, a 1948 Texas court decision that forced schools to stop choosing specific buildings in their districts to be for Mexican students only, and *Hernandez v. State of Texas*, a 1954 U.S. Supreme Court decision that said the discriminatory laws affecting African Americans could not be applied to Mexican Americans.

Looking
to the Future

Renata's smile as she walked away from the children was genuine. They were so sweet and so hopeful that she couldn't help but feel a lift, in spite of their tough situation. She knew they were the future of the Hispanic American civil rights movement. Without them, her people would go nowhere. Even though their schooling might be limited, activism at such a young age could teach a powerful lesson. She looked over her shoulder at the huge crowd of people gathered and was amazed at the sheer number. Hispanic Americans filled the area as far as she could see. Children were playing. Adults were standing and talking. Even grandmothers and grandfathers were milling about. She knew that this was a good sign, a sign of things to come for her people. It was the perfect scene for her final shoot of the day.

Latinos at a street celebration

"This is Renata Hernandez reporting live from Washington D.C. Behind me you can see the scores of people here this afternoon to raise public awareness of the problems facing Hispanic people across the country. Today I have interviewed people of all ages, from all walks of life, and from all parts of the nation. Hispanic Americans have been a vital part of this country since the time of the Treaty of Guadalupe Hidalgo and even before that, and we deserve equal treatment. We deserve equal treatment at work. We deserve the right to own good homes. We deserve equal treatment at schools. We deserve equal treatment in government. The point is: it is time for a change America! These people behind me are doing their part. Don't forget to do yours! This is Renata Hernandez for Teledia, signing off."

The Largest Minority

Although the protest described in our story is not real, the sentiments expressed by the characters are very real. Hispanic Americans have become the nation's largest minority group. Already, Hispanic culture is so dominant that salsa has replaced ketchup as the nation's number-one condiment for foods. Congress has established Hispanic Heritage Month, recognized nationally September 15 through October 15 each year, to honor and promote awareness of the culture and diversity brought to the country by the people from the twenty-two nations that have come to be recognized under the term "Hispanic." Whether people like it or not, Hispanic Americans are changing the country.

Due to the way immigration laws are written, the majority of the Hispanic American population will be native-born U.S. citizens by the year 2030. Any individual born on United States soil is granted automatic citizenship, and Hispanics have a higher birthrate than any other ethnic group. With increased citizenship, Hispanic Americans will have a greater amount of political power, but along with this power comes responsibility. Hispanic America's leadership will have the responsibility to shape governmental policy to protect their culture and to further the gains made during the last century.

undreds of organizations across the United States continue the work of the civil rights movement. The National Council of La Raza (NCLR) is a private, non-profit organization established to reduce poverty and discrimination, and improve life opportunities for Hispanics. NCLR is the nation's largest *constituency*-based Hispanic organization serving all Hispanic nationality groups in all regions of the country. The organization works through a formal network of affiliates and a broader network of more than 20,000 groups and individuals nationwide. It reaches more than 3 million Latinos annually.

constituency: *a group of people thought to have common goals or views.*

The Most Critical Factor

ducation is perhaps the most critical factor to the success of Hispanic Americans across the country. A strong education can serve as a springboard for bigger and better things. In order to attain equality, Hispanic Americans need to level the playing field in employment and education. To get the high-

Recent immigrants in Miami wait for assistance at Church World Service,
an agency that provides job training, English classes, and other services.

postsecondary education: courses or educational programs designed for learners who have completed high school or its equivalent.

Hispanic Serving Institutions: higher education institutions that have been awarded grants to expand their capacity to serve Hispanic and low-income students.

paying jobs, a *postsecondary* education is a must. An increase in education will likely equal an increase in income and voter presence at the polls. The future of education in the country is very important to Hispanic Americans, who have the most to gain by the implementation of good education policies.

Throughout the country, Hispanic Americans are calling for programs that improve the success of educational programs for Hispanic youths. Family outreach policies that encourage enrollment in early childhood programs will help pave the way for improved educational outcomes in the future. The formative pre-kindergarten years can have a huge impact on education, and getting started early is the key.

Increasing Hispanic participation in gifted and talented programs will help improve the ability and desire of these students to attend college. Such programs are excellent indicators of future educational performance.

Among U.S. colleges and universities, there are currently about 250 that have been designated *Hispanic Serving Institutions* (HSIs) by the federal government. To qualify as an HSI, a college must list at least half of its students as having come from low-income backgrounds, and at least one quarter of the students have to be Hispanic in origin. The list of HSIs has grown by about fifteen colleges each year since 1992, when the designation was first established. HSIs receive federal money for their acceptance of Hispanic students and usually market their college directly to Hispanic students in city schools. The HSI program has helped increase enrollment of Hispanic students in higher education, but there is certainly room for improvement. Across the country, increasing numbers of colleges are adopting classes that are more attentive to Hispanic needs in an effort to tap into the rapidly growing pool of potential students.

Disturbingly, there are several recent trends that make it very

The Youth Co-op in Miami assists Hispanic immigrants.

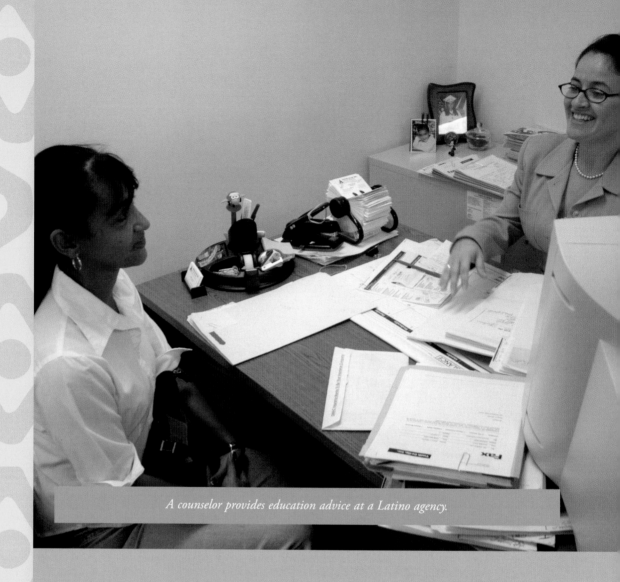

A counselor provides education advice at a Latino agency.

difficult for Hispanic American students to attend college. Year after year, public colleges and universities have had to increase tuition to meet their operating costs as federal and state aid has failed to cover the gap. Increases in tuition hit poor students hard. Wary of taking loans, Hispanic students find it very difficult to make ends meet, and their academic performance suffers as they work as many as three jobs just to pay tuition, while maintaining a full course load. There has been a shift in financial aid away from grants, which are not repaid, to student loans. The effect has been to drive down Hispanic enrollment. There is a belief that more Hispanic students would attend college if they could do so without building large amounts of debt, but in recent years, that is not possible. Hispanic students from poor neighborhoods are afraid to take on loans because they are fighting to get out of the debt that has surrounded them their whole lives.

Many colleges and universities in the urban areas of the country have resorted to placing enrollment caps on their incoming classes in an effort to keep class sizes and costs down. Hispanic students are more likely to be turned away than any other ethnic group, in part because of their poor performance on standardized tests and admission exams. Colleges prefer to accept students whose scores on these tests are high, because they can use the scores to compare their student population with that of other colleges. Being able to say that their students have higher test scores than some other college can attract more highly educated students, and every college in the nation wants to be able to say they have the smartest student body. Unfortunately, this practice excludes many Hispanic Americans.

socioeconomic status: a division of population based on occupation, income, and education.

Affirmative action has been very helpful to Hispanics, especially in college enrollment practices. Colleges and universities have been required to admit a certain number of minority students, which has greatly benefited Hispanic Americans seeking to enroll in colleges. Recently, affirmative action has been under political and legal attack, and as a result, has been weakened severely. At colleges where affirmative action has been reduced or eliminated, Hispanic enrollment has declined rapidly. This does not mean that all colleges are turning their backs on Hispanic students. Some colleges have turned to using *socioeconomic status* rather than ethnic background as a key factor in determining enrollment. A certain percentage of their students are from poor neighborhoods, and often these students are Hispanic. This type of policy is relatively new and unproven. It remains to be seen how well it works.

resently, the future of education for Hispanic Americans is largely in the hands of non-Hispanics. As evidenced by the changes in California, the movement toward the establishment of English as the official language of the United States seems to be an issue that will not go quietly. Interestingly, the majority of Hispanics in the state supported the proposition. Most Hispanic Americans feel that English is the language of success in the United States, and they want their children to be confident speakers in social situations. The federal government expends nearly $400 million per year to support bilingual programs across the country, an expense that surely gets the attention of lawmakers seeking ways to trim dollars from federal expenses. Time will tell whether other states are willing and able to follow California's lead on bilingual education.

One of the other keys to the future for Hispanic Americans in the United States is unification. There are millions of Hispanics in the country, spread across every state of the nation. That they are spread out tends to weaken their influence in any one region, so Hispanics must unite to make their case known. A number of relatively large and well-developed Hispanic organizations seek to do just this. As they grow in size, these organizations also invariably grow in political power. Being able to reach thousands of Hispanic voters and unify them at election time is one of the benefits of such organization. Politicians, presidential candidates in particular, are very aware of the power of the Hispanic vote, as evidenced by the amount of campaigning they target toward Hispanic voters. To gain power, the voters have to consider carefully the candidates and their messages, and vote for the individual who will best suit their needs. The vote is a powerful tool in a democracy, and Hispanics must find a way to tap into the power of their numbers to influence policymakers. Hispanics have the ability to influence seriously the outcome of presidential elections in ten states that are critical to a candidate's bid for the White House.

If Latino citizens exercise their privilege to vote, they could become a powerful political force.

Voter registration

Hispanics must also gain representation in government at all levels. They are woefully underrepresented in federal elected positions and must strive to use their power as voters to change the face of the House of Representatives, Senate, and the presidency. Ideally, Hispanics will be able to increase their numbers at all levels of government. As their numbers continue to increase, it will not be long before Hispanic Americans hold many key positions in government.

As Hispanic presence in government increases, discrimination is likely to decrease. New policies will be created that will help reduce or eliminate the poor treatment of Hispanic Americans in all aspects of life. Currently, Hispanics hold only twenty-five seats in the House of Representatives, and none in the Senate. This represents an increase of six seats since 2000, a modest increase. Hispanics seeking equality should push for more representation in the Congress and Senate.

When asked if he wanted to be remembered with statues and memorials, the great civil rights activist César Chávez replied, "If you want to remember, organize!"

he Future Leader of America (FLA) is an organization that promotes the development of leadership skills and an understanding of the political system to Hispanic youths. FLA recruits fourteen- and fifteen-year-old Latino students from California and Mexico for entry-level programs. Many major California and Mexico universities offer one- and two-day seminars for the students.

Habla Español

futura (foo-too-rah): future

esperanza (ace-pare-on-sah): hope

Timeline

1776—The Declaration of Independence written.

1848—The United States and Mexico sign the Treaty of Guadalupe Hidalgo.

1927—League of United Latin American Citizens (LULAC) organizes in Texas.

October 29, 1929—Black Tuesday, the beginning of the Great Depression.

1954—U.S. Supreme Court rules on *Brown v. Board of Education (Topeka, Kansas)*.

1960—United Farm Workers Association (NFWA) established.

1965—The NFWA organizes the grape boycott.

1965—U.S. government establishes the Equal Employment Opportunity Commission.

1965—Voting Rights Act passes Congress.

1968—Civil Rights Act passes Congress.

Further Reading

Cardenas, Gilberto. *La Causa: Civil Rights, Social Justice and the Struggle for Equality in the Midwest*. Houston, Tex.: Arte Publico Press, 2004.

Chavez, Linda. *Out of the Barrio: Toward a New Politics of Hispanic Assimilation*. New York: Basic Books, 1992.

DeFreitas, Gregory Flanery. *Inequality at Work: Hispanics in the U.S. Labor Force*. New York: Oxford University Press, 1991.

Freedman, Russell. *In Defense of Liberty: The Story of America's Bill of Rights*. New York: Holiday House, 2003.

Gastil, Raymond D. and Leonard R. Sussman. *Freedom in the World: Political Rights and Civil Liberties, 1986–1987*. New York: Greenwood Press, 1987.

Kly, Y. N. *A Popular Guide to Minority Rights*. Atlanta: Clarity Press, 1995.

Levy, Debbie. *Civil Liberties*. San Diego, Calif.: Greenhaven Press, 2000.

Levy, Peter. *Let Freedom Ring: A Documentary History of the Modern Civil Rights Movement*. Westport, Conn.: Praeger, 1992.

Patrick, John. *The Bill of Rights: A History in Documents*. New York: Oxford University Press, 2003.

Rosales, F. Arturo. *Chicano! The History of the Mexican American Civil Rights Movement*. Houston, Tex.: Arte Publico Press, 1996.

Waller, James. *Face to Face: The Changing State of Racism across America*. New York: Insight Books, 1998.

Williams, John B. *Race Discrimination in Public Higher Education: Interpreting Federal Civil Rights Enforcement, 1964–1996*. Westport, Conn.: Praeger Paperback, 1997.

For More Information

Affirmative Action for African, Hispanic (Latino), and Asian Americans
http://www.ethnicmajority.com/affirmative_action.htm

CMMR – Latino/Hispanic Resources
http://wwwrcf.usc.edu/~cmmr/Latino.html

Civil Rights Coalition for the 21st Century
http://www.civilrights.org/

Civil Rights - Law & History
http://www.usdoj.gov/kidspage/crt/crtmenu.htm

Dolores Huertas: Labor Leader with a Passion for Justice
http://www.nwhp.org/tlp/biographies/huerta/huerta_bio.html

Fight in the Fields: Cesar Chavez and the Farmworkers Struggle
http://www.pbs.org/itvs/fightfields/

Hispanic Americans: Census Facts
http://www.factmonster.com/spot/hhmcensus1.html

Hispanic Heritage Plaza
http://www.hispaniconline.com/hh/timeline/index.html

Latin Business Association
http://www.lbausa.com/

NCLR – Civil Rights for Hispanic Americans
http://www2.nclr.forumone.com/policy/civil.html

NOAA Civil Rights Office
http://www.ofa.noaa.gov/~civilr/hisppage.htm

Our Nation on the Fault Line: Hispanic American Education
http://www.ed.gov/pubs/FaultLine/who.html

United Farmworkers Union
http://www.ufw.org/

Voices of Civil Rights
http://www.voicesofcivilrights.org/history.html

Publisher's note:

The Web sites listed on this page were active at the time of publication. The publisher is not responsible for Web sites that have changed their addresses or discontinued operation since the date of publication. The publisher will review and update the Web site list upon each reprint.

Index

Picture Credits

Benjamin Stewart: pp. 18, 24, 44, 58, 67, 71, 72, 78, 93, 97, 99, 100

Carin Zissis, carinzissis@hotmail.com: p. 88

Centro Library and Archives, Centro de Estudios Puertorriqueños, Hunter College, CUNY, Photographer unknown: p. 46

Charles A. Hack: pp. 11, 17, 83, 94

Dover: p. 15

The Justo A. Martí Photographic Collection, Centro de Estudios Puertorriqueños, Hunter College, CUNY, Photographer unknown: pp. 48, 61, 104

Library of Congress: pp. 29, 33

The National Archives and Records Administration: pp. 35, 77

PhotoDisc: pp. 82, 103

Photos.com: pp. 12, 16, 36

The Records of the Offices of the Government of Puerto Rico in the U.S., Centro de Estudios Puertorriqueños, Hunter College, CUNY, Photographer unknown: pp. 27, 30, 57, 63, 87

The Ruth M. Reynolds Papers, Centro de Estudios Puertorriqueños, Hunter College, CUNY, Photographer unknown: pp. 9, 43, 84

Santiago Iglesias, Centro de Estudios Puertorriqueños, Hunter College, CUNY, Photographer unknown: pp. 21, 23

Biographies

Miranda Hunter lives in a small town in western New York. Miranda studied political science at Geneva College and law at the University at Buffalo School of Law. She's had a passion for all things right and fair from a very early age and decided to pursue that by studying law. Miranda has recently changed careers to become a high school teacher.

Dr. José E. Limón is professor of Mexican-American Studies at the University of Texas at Austin where he has taught for twenty-five years. He has authored over forty articles and three books on Latino cultural studies and history. He lectures widely to academic audiences, civic groups, and K–12 educators.